Blue Whales

and Other Baleen Whales

Book Author: Christina Johnson
For World Book:
Editorial: Paul A. Kobasa, Maureen Liebenson, Scott Richardson, Christine Sullivan
Research: Andy Roberts, Loranne Shields
Graphics and Design: Melanie Bender, Sandra Dyrlund
Photos: Tom Evans, Sylvia Ohlrich
Permissions: Janet Peterson
Indexing: David Pofelski
Proofreading: Anne Dillon
Pre-press and Manufacturing: Carma Fazio, Anne Fritzinger, Steve Hueppchen, Madelyn Underwood

**For information about other World Book publications, visit our Web site at
http://www.worldbook.com, or call 1-800-WORLDBK (967-5325).**

**For information about sales to schools and libraries, call 1-800-975-3250 (United States);
1-800-837-5365 (Canada).**

World Book, Inc.
233 N. Michigan Avenue
Chicago, IL 60601
U.S.A.

Library of Congress Cataloging-in-Publication Data

Blue whales and other baleen whales.
        p. cm. — (World Book's animals of the world)
    Includes bibliographical references (p.).
    ISBN 0-7166-1264-X — ISBN 0-7166-1261-5
        1. Baleen whales—Juvenile literature. 2. Blue whales—Juvenile literature.
    I. World Book, Inc. II. Series.

    QL737 .C42B58 2005
    599.5'2—dc22
                                        2004011341
Printed in Malaysia
1 2 3 4 5 6 7 8 09 08 07 06 05

Picture Acknowledgments: Cover: © Kelvin Aitken, Visual & Written/Bruce Coleman Inc.; © Phillip Colla, SeaPics.com;
© Wolfgang Kaehler, Corbis; © Doug Perrine, HWRF/NMFS permit #587/SeaPics.com; © Doug Perrine, SeaPics.com.

© Kelvin Aitken, Visual & Written/Bruce Coleman Inc. 4, 45; © Phillip Colla, Ocean Light 29; © Phillip Colla, SeaPics.com 27;
© Graeme Ellis, Ursus Photography 43; © John Ford, Ursus Photography 47; © Francois Gohier 11, 37; © Wolcott Henry,
National Geographic Image Collection 41; © Peter Howorth, Norbert Wu Productions 61; © John Hyde, Bruce Coleman Inc. 35;
© Wolfgang Kaehler, Corbis 57; © Flip Nicklin, NMFS permit #987/Minden Pictures 33; © Michael Nolan, SeaPics.com 5, 39;
© Doug Perrine, HWRF/NMFS permit #587/SeaPics.com 51; © Doug Perrine, SeaPics.com 31; © Robert Pitman, SeaPics.com
17; © Stig Thormodsrud, stigphoto.com 3, 7; © David Tipling, Photographer's Choice/Getty Images 19; © Masa Ushioda,
SeaPics.com 5, 25, 59; © Tom Walmsley, Nature Picture Library 23; © James Watt, Animals Animals 53; © Jim Watt, Bruce
Coleman Collection 49; © Doc White, SeaPics.com 21; © Norbert Wu, Norbert Wu Productions 55.

Illustrations: WORLD BOOK illustrations by John Fleck 13, 15.

World Book's Animals of the World

Blue Whales
and Other Baleen Whales

Do you think there were dinosaurs bigger than me?

World Book, Inc.
a Scott Fetzer company
Chicago

Contents

What Is a Whale? 6

Where in the World Do Blue Whales and Other Baleens Live? 8

How Can You Tell It's a Baleen Whale? 10

What Is Under All That Blubber? 12

Just How Big Are Blue Whales Anyway? 14

Are All Baleen Whales Huge? 16

What Do Blue Whales Eat to Get So Big? 18

Why Are Blue Whales Called Gulpers? 20

Do Blue Whales Get Cold or Hot? 22

Does a Blue Whale Have a Good Sense of
Sight, Hearing, Touch, and Smell? 24

Do Blue Whales Have Enemies? 26

What Is a Baby Blue Whale's Life Like? 28

Do Whales Have Belly Buttons? 30

Are Blue Whales and Other Baleens Social Animals? 32

Do Blue Whales Have Any Relatives on Land? 34

What Is Spouting? 36

Don't try to put any bow on my head!

I've got my eye on you!

How Do Whales Communicate?.....................38

Do Whales Drink Water? 40

Do Baleen Whales Sleep? 42

What Colors Are Baleen Whales? 44

What Is a Bubble Net?............................46

Which Whale Serenades Its Mate?.................48

Which Whale Is Known for Its "Wings"? 50

Which Whales Have the Longest Baleens? 52

Which Whale Migrates Off the West Coast
of the United States?............................54

Which Whale Moves the Fastest?..................56

How Do Scientists Study Whales?.................58

Are Baleen Whales in Danger? 60

Baleen Whale Fun Facts 62

Glossary 63

Index/Baleen Whale Classification 64

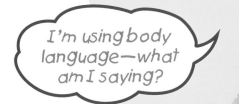

I'm using body language—what am I saying?

What Is a Whale?

A whale is a marine mammal with a layer of fat, called blubber, flippers, a long tail, and a blowhole. There are two kinds of whales: toothed whales and baleen *(buh LEEN)* whales. A toothed whale has teeth—belugas, porpoises, and dolphins are all toothed whales. Instead of teeth, a baleen whale has hundreds of hairy plates hanging from its massive upper jaw. These plates are called baleen, and they are made up of the same material that makes up human fingernails.

Like other mammals, baleen whales breathe air, are warm-blooded, and give birth to live young. Unlike most mammals, however, baleen whales spend their entire lives in the ocean. What really distinguishes baleen whales from other life on Earth is their enormous size.

All the largest whales are baleen whales. The blue whale you see here is the largest of all. It belongs to the family of baleen whales called rorquals *(RAWR kwuhls)*. Rorquals have long ridges on their throats. Humpback, fin, minke *(MIHNG kee),* and sei *(say)* whales are rorquals. The three other baleen families are gray whales, bowhead and right whales, and pygmy right whales.

Blue whale breaching

7

Where in the World Do Blue Whales and Other Baleens Live?

Some baleens, for example, blue whales, live in all the oceans. Their summer feeding areas are in or near the waters of the cold polar regions. In winter, blue whales and the other baleen whales that live in the polar regions migrate to breed and give birth in the comforting warmth of the tropics. Sometimes migrating whales travel thousands of miles between their winter and summer habitats.

Some baleen whales, however, do not migrate. Bowhead whales, for example, never leave the Arctic Ocean, while Bryde's whales spend their entire lives in warm tropical and subtropical waters.

World Map

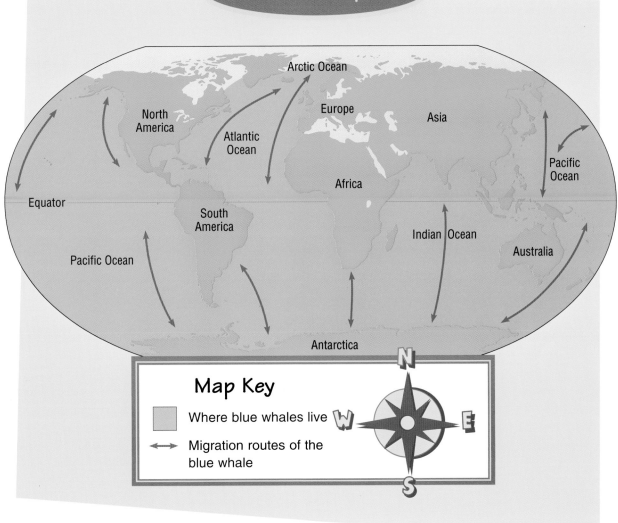

Arctic Ocean

Europe

Asia

North
America

Atlantic
Ocean

Africa

Pacific
Ocean

Equator

South
America

Indian Ocean

Australia

Pacific Ocean

Antarctica

Map Key

Where blue whales live

Migration routes of the
blue whale

N
W   E
S

9

How Can You Tell It's a Baleen Whale?

You can tell a shark or a large fish from either kind of whale by watching how the animal's tail moves. Sharks and other large fish move their tails from side to side when they swim. They "snake" through the water. But, a whale pushes itself through the water by moving its tail up and down.

If the animal moves its tail up and down and makes quick movements through the water, then it is probably a dolphin or other type of toothed whale. A baleen whale is not as agile as these animals. And, baleen whales usually are much larger than toothed whales.

You can also identify a baleen whale by its blowholes. A baleen whale has two blowholes on the top of its head. Dolphins and other toothed whales have one.

Of course, it's easy to tell a baleen whale if its mouth is open. Just look for the baleen plates!

Humpback whale

What Is Under All That Blubber?

Blubber is the layer of fat under a whale's skin. Under all their blubber, whales are a lot like other mammals. Their nervous, digestive, and circulatory systems are very much like those of other mammals.

Their brain is highly complex and encased in a hard skull that is connected to a spinal cord. They have a stomach and intestines through which food is processed and a heart that pumps blood.

Whales are also wonderfully adapted to life in the sea. Because of their size, shape, and blubber, they are able to keep warm, even in the frigid polar oceans. And, they can store huge amounts of oxygen in their blood and muscles, so they are able to stay underwater for a very long time.

Baleen whales have bony skeletons, but their lightweight bones would not be strong enough to support them if they lived on land. The seawater that surrounds them helps to support their large bodies.

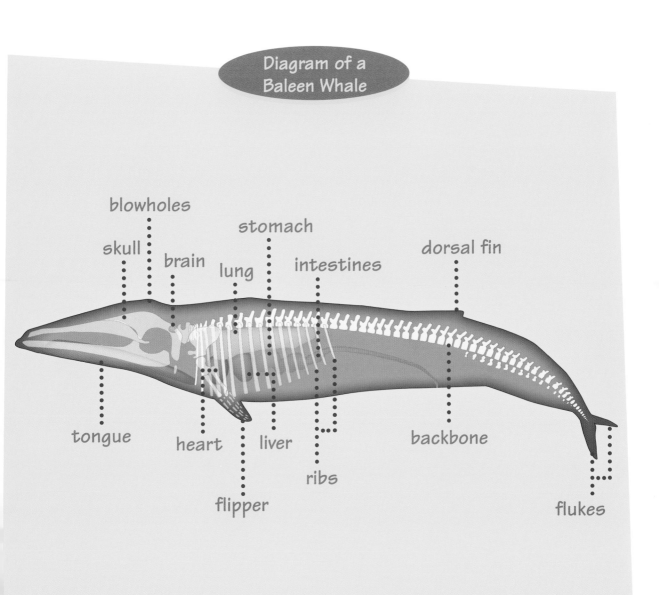

Diagram of a Baleen Whale

blowholes

skull

brain

lung

stomach

intestines

dorsal fin

tongue

heart

liver

backbone

ribs

flipper

flukes

13

EAU CLAIRE DISTRICT LIBRARY

Just How Big Are Blue Whales Anyway?

A blue whale's heart is the size of a small car. Its tongue weighs as much as an elephant. A toddler could easily fit into one of its blowholes. A single blue whale is heavier than a group of 1,600 average-sized people.

Blue whales are not just big, they are absolutely, incredibly, and astoundingly huge—bigger than any dinosaur that ever lived. A blue whale can reach 100 feet (30 meters) in length and may tip the scales at 300,000 pounds (136,000 kilograms).

As with all baleen whales, female blue whales are larger than males.

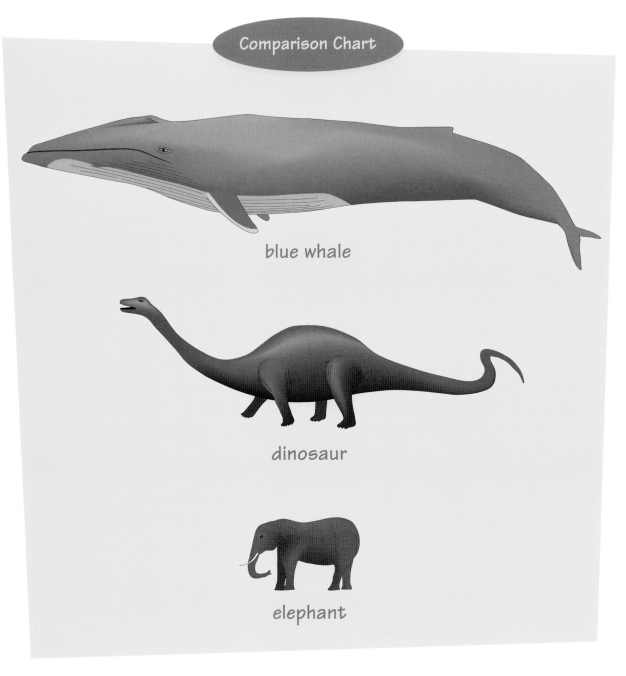

blue whale

dinosaur

elephant

Are All Baleen Whales Huge?

Not all baleen whales are huge. But compared with animals on land, even a small baleen whale is big.

The pygmy right whale is the smallest baleen whale. Females reach lengths of about 20 feet (6 meters) and can weigh 7,500 pounds (3,400 kilograms). This is still quite a bit larger than a hippopotamus, for example, which weighs up to 5,800 pounds (2,630 kilograms).

Besides being relatively small, pygmy whales are mysterious. People rarely see them. Dead pygmy whales have washed up on Australian, South African, and South American shores, leading scientists to think pygmy whales probably live south of the equator. But this is only a guess. Scientists know very little about the range of pygmy whales or where they feed and breed.

The next smallest baleen whale is the minke whale. Minke whales grow to be about 33 feet (10 meters) long and may weigh up to 20,000 pounds (9,100 kilograms).

All the other baleen whales are longer than 40 feet (12 meters). Because baleen whales are so big, they are sometimes referred to as "the great whales."

Pygmy right whale

What Do Blue Whales Eat to Get So Big?

Krill for breakfast. Krill for lunch. Krill for dinner. Blue whales that spend the summer months in cold polar waters eat a whole lot of one thing—krill.

Krill resemble shrimp. They have long antennae, dark eyes, and delicate, almost transparent (see-through), bodies. Some kinds of krill are much smaller than the shrimp people eat. These krill, which are the type blue whales eat, have bodies about half as long as a penny is across.

Krill make good whale food because of their abundance and high nutritional value. Pound for pound, krill contain as much protein as red meat, and they contain all the energy, trace minerals, and vitamins that blue whales require.

It does, however, take a lot of krill to fill a hungry whale. During the summer feeding season, a blue whale may devour over 10,000 pounds (4,536 kilograms) of krill a day.

A close-up view of
Antarctic krill

Why Are Blue Whales Called Gulpers?

When blue whales feed, they take huge gulps of water. For this reason, they are called gulpers.

Like all rorqual whales, blue whales have pleats on their throat that expand just like an accordion. By gulping, they transform their throat into a giant pouch. By pressing their tongue against their baleen, the whales squeeze out the water. Then they eat the krill that remain trapped against the baleen.

Humpback, sei, minke, and fin whales are also "gulpers." Right whales and bowhead whales, however, are "skimmers." They swim slowly near the sea surface, continuously straining seawater through their baleen.

The gray whale is different from all the other baleen whales in its feeding habits. Gray whales eat the tiny animals from the mud and sand on the floor of the ocean. To do this, the whales plow the bottom of the sea with their heads and suck up huge scoops of muck.

A blue whale
feeding on krill

Do Blue Whales Get Cold or Hot?

Blue whales inhabit some of the coldest waters and some of the warmest waters on the planet. Yet, they maintain a constant body temperature of about 98 degrees Fahrenheit (36.6 degrees Celsius), nearly the same as our body temperature of 98.6 degrees Fahrenheit (37 degrees Celsius).

Amazingly, blue whales are so well adapted for cold temperatures that it is easy for them to keep warm in cold waters. The shape and large size of a blue whale's body help it to retain heat. Normally, a blue whale has very little blood in its body's outer layers, and this also helps the whale to keep body heat inside.

Blue whales actually have a harder time getting rid of excess heat. So, unlike other whales, they don't need as thick a layer of blubber. A blue whale's blubber is only 6 inches (15 centimeters) thick, whereas some other whales are covered in a 20-inch (51-centimeter) layer. A blue whale may get rid of excess heat by sending more blood than normal to its skin surface, which cools the whale's blood.

A blue whale
spraying a sea bird

Does a Blue Whale Have a Good Sense of Sight, Hearing, Touch, and Smell?

Blue whales and other baleen whales have good eyesight. Unlike the round eyes of humans, however, baleen whales have eyes that are flattened in the front. This eye shape is better for seeing in a dim, underwater habitat.

Baleen whales also have amazing hearing. They hear sounds that are inaudible to humans. A whale's ear doesn't look like it would be so sensitive to sound. Its ear looks like a tiny hole in the side of its head. There is no ear lobe or outer ear.

Touch is another sense that is very well developed in these whales. A baleen whale's skin is very sensitive to touch.

Though whales can see, hear, and feel, scientists are not certain if they have any sense of smell.

Close view of the eye
of a humpback whale

Do Blue Whales Have Enemies?

An animal as large as a blue whale has few natural enemies. Only diseased or young blue whales are at risk of being attacked by sharks or killer whales.

Newborn whales are the most vulnerable because they are small and swim slowly. Mother whales swim beside their young, shielding them from predators.

If a group of killer whales targets a young whale, however, it is a challenge to protect it. Lacking teeth, claws, or tusks, blue whales have only their size—and powerful tail—to ward off attack. Killer whales will rip small chunks of flesh from a young or sick whale until it finally dies.

It is humans, however, and not killer whales, that have been the most dangerous enemy of blue whales. Hunting and water pollution have killed many whales.

Blue whale
mother with calf

What Is a Baby Blue Whale's Life Like?

For the first year or so, a calf stays with its mother. After that, it is independent. Though blue whales don't have a long childhood, blue whale mothers are very attentive while they care for their young. A mother never leaves her young calf until the calf is ready to set out on its own.

Eating is an important part of a young blue whale's life. A newborn calf weighs about 6,000 pounds (2,700 kilograms). Nursing on its mother's fatty milk, it gains about 200 pounds (90 kilograms) a day. By the time it is 7 months old, it will be about 50 feet (15 meters) long and will weigh about 46,000 pounds (21,000 kilograms)—it is then ready to begin feeding on krill.

Nursing a young whale is extremely taxing on a mother whale. A mother whale may lose as much as 100,000 pounds (45,400 kilograms), possibly as much as one-third of her body weight, while nursing.

Blue whale calf with mother

Do Whales Have Belly Buttons?

Like other mammals, female baleen whales give birth to live young. Baby whales grow inside their mother's womb and receive oxygen and vital nutrients through the umbilical cord, which is attached to their mother's circulatory system.

The umbilical cord on a human baby is cut after a baby is born. The umbilical cord of a baleen whale breaks automatically as a calf's head emerges from its mother's body during the birth process. Whales are usually born fluke—or tail—first, unlike people, who most often come out head first. The place where the umbilical cord was once attached to the baby is called the navel, or belly button. So, yes, whales have belly buttons, too.

Sei whale calf

Are Blue Whales and Other Baleens Social Animals?

After a blue whale calf separates from its mother, a blue whale will spend most of its time alone. Blue whales are rarely seen in the large groups that are common to dolphins, killer whales, and other toothed whales.

Biologists sometimes see pairs of blue whales swimming and feeding together. These pairs will usually consist of a female and a male, or a female and its calf.

Like the blue whale, most other baleen whales spend much of their time alone. However, humpback, right, and gray whales are known to form small groups. These groups may contain a dozen or so whales feeding and traveling together.

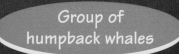

Group of
humpback whales

Do Blue Whales Have Any Relatives on Land?

You may be surprised to learn that a blue whale's closest living relatives on land include pigs, deer, and hippopotamuses. The first whales, which appeared more than 50 million years ago, had evolved from primitive hoofed mammals.

The early ancestors of whales had teeth, lived on land, and had four legs that ended in hoofs. They foraged for food in shallow coastal waters. Slowly, over millions of years, the body shape of these animals changed. Front legs developed into flippers. Back legs disappeared. The nostrils moved to the back of the snout, becoming blowholes.

Amazingly, even modern whales show traces of their origins as walking land mammals. Baleen whales have tiny hipbones, which are all that remain of their back legs. And, a baleen whale fetus has teeth while it develops inside its mother. These teeth disappear before birth.

Blue whale flukes

What Is Spouting?

When a whale is swimming underwater, it is holding its breath. Try holding your breath for a moment. Soon you will want to resume breathing. How do you do this? You exhale. Only then can you inhale new air. Whales do the same, but they are much better at storing oxygen in their bodies than are humans. So, they can go longer periods between breaths.

When a whale exhales, it ejects a powerful blast of moist air. This is called a spout or a blow. The whale you see here is spouting.

Different species of whales have differently shaped spouts. The spout of a right whale, for example, is shaped like a giant V, while that of a gray whale looks like a single, broad cloud of mist.

Blue whale spouting

How Do Whales Communicate?

Baleen whales communicate with sounds and their bodies. Many baleen whales, including blue whales, make low-pitched calls that humans cannot hear. These vocalizations can travel hundreds of miles. The true function of these long-distance calls is unknown, but scientists think they allow whales to communicate even when they cannot see each other. Vocalizations are probably used in courtship and perhaps to navigate during migration.

Body language also is an important means of communicating. Whales may breach—leap out of the water—to express aggression or distress, or calves will do it out of playfulness. Another common form of body language whales use is slapping their tail on the surface—this behavior is called lobtailing. A whale may use this signal as a warning, or to let other whales know of its location in the water.

Humpback whale
lobtailing

39

Do Whales Drink Water?

Like people, baleen whales don't drink salt water. Salt water is harmful to them the same way it is harmful to us. Salt water causes dehydration—that is, an excessive loss of water from the body. Seals, sea lions, toothed and baleen whales—all marine mammals get water from foods they eat. Like most animals, the krill and fish that whales eat are mostly made up of water. A fish is a great source of water for a whale, because the water in a fish's body isn't salty. Krill, however, is quite salty. But whales have kidneys that are especially adapted to separating out the excess salt that enters the whales' blood from its food. This salt is then released in their urine.

A whale's blubber layer is another source of water. When whales do not have access to food, they "drink" what they need from their blubber stores. A thin whale risks not only starvation, but also dying of thirst.

A blue whale
viewed from above

Do Baleen Whales Sleep?

Baleen whales do sleep, but scientists know very little about how they sleep. And, they can't sleep deeply the way people and other land mammals do. Whales must come to the surface of the water to breathe, so they can't stay motionless in the water for long periods.

The brain of a baleen whale, like the human brain, has two sides—a right and a left hemisphere.

When a whale sleeps, scientists think only one side of the brain rests at a time. The other side stays awake to direct the whale to the surface for air. By letting one side of the brain rest, whales catch a nap without drowning. Both baleen whales and toothed whales sleep with half a brain awake.

When sleeping, whales sometimes position themselves near the water's surface so they can pop up easily for air.

Humpback whale near the water's surface

What Colors Are Baleen Whales?

Baleen whales are not colorful animals. They do not come in the vibrant purples, reds, greens, and yellows of tropical fish. Most whales are different shades of gray. Typically, a baleen whale has a dark gray back and a lighter gray underside.

Blue whales look blue underwater but actually are speckled blue-gray and white. Tiny yellow organisms sometimes grow on their undersides, making their bellies look yellow. These tiny organisms do not affect the whale at all.

Gray whales are gray with lots of white splotches. These splotches are not their natural skin coloring; they are caused by barnacles and other organisms growing on their skin. A barnacle is a small, round shellfish commonly found on boat hulls.

Humpback whales are black on top and white underneath. Bowhead and right whales are nearly all black.

Bowhead whale

What Is a Bubble Net?

Humpback whales eat a variety of foods, including many kinds of krill and small fish that live in groups called schools. To help drive large amounts of krill and fish into small, easy-to-eat clusters, humpback whales make nets by blowing bubbles. To make a bubble net, a humpback whale first dives beneath a school of fish or krill. It then blows columns of bubbles as it circles below. Slowly, it spirals upward around the prey, creating a cylinder of bubbles with its prey trapped inside.

When the net is complete, the whale will open its mouth wide and lunge at the center of its bubble net. Often, several humpbacks will work together—one makes the bubble net while the others feed.

Humpback whales using
a bubble net to feed

47

Which Whale Serenades Its Mate?

Birds, insects, and frogs all sing. And, so do humpback whales.

Male humpbacks are the opera singers of the ocean. A male humpback may growl, moan, whine, and make violinlike sounds, repeating the sounds in the same order continuously for hours, sometimes days. Portions of a song may be heard from hundreds of miles away by other whales.

Males sing during the breeding season. For this reason, biologists think the songs are meant to woo potential mates. They may also help to keep other males away.

Males from the same region sing a similar tune. So, it would seem a male whale learns his song from the other males in his area. Each male, however, modifies his song slowly over time, making it unique— yet it is still recognizable as a song of his group.

A male and a female humpback whale

Which Whale Is Known for Its "Wings"?

Humpback whales have very long flippers, longer than any other baleen whale. They are so long that they look like small airplane wings. Measured from the body of the whale to the tip of the flipper, a flipper can be 17 feet (5 meters) in length.

Most of the time, humpback whales use their flippers as giant paddles. Flippers help the whale steer and balance while swimming.

Sometimes though, it looks as if flippers could be used as wings. Humpback whales are the most acrobatic of all the baleen whales. They often hurl themselves out of the water head first. For a brief second, you think they really will fly. But, of course, they don't, and they splash back into the ocean. Humpbacks also like to slap their tails on the surface, making loud sounds and giant splashes.

Humpback whale breaching

Which Whales Have the Longest Baleens?

Bowhead and right whales have the longest baleens. These whales are rounder and fatter than blue whales, and they have huge heads. The baleen of these whales can be 7 to 13 feet (2 to 4 meters) long. Huge strands of baleen let a right whale strain greater volumes of water as it feeds. Instead of gulping water, as do blue whales, bowhead and right whales swim slowly with their mouths open and catch tiny floating organisms called copepods.

Right whales swim so slowly that barnacles and other small organisms are able to live on their skin. The barnacles survive by capturing and eating other tiny organisms floating in the water. Other types of organisms, such as whale lice, feed on the whale's skin. Luckily for the whales, these whale lice don't appear to cause much harm. Right whales usually have patches of organisms growing on their face. So do some other baleen whales, such as humpback and gray whales.

Right whale showing
its baleen

Which Whale Migrates Off the West Coast of the United States?

Gray whales migrate between the Bering Sea off Alaska and the shallow bays of Baja California, Mexico. During their migration, they swim along the coasts of Alaska, Washington, Oregon, and California.

Their migration is one of the longest in the animal kingdom. Some gray whales swim 5,000 miles (8,000 kilometers) one way. The females are especially impressive because they make one migration journey while pregnant and another soon after giving birth.

Because they feed on bottom animals, gray whales stay closer to shore than other whales. For this reason, whale watchers on the West Coast often see more gray whales than other species, such as blue whales.

Gray whales used to live off the East Coast of the United States. That population is now extinct. Today, a small population still lives off the coast of Asia, and these whales migrate between the coasts of Russia and southern China.

54

Gray whales off the
coast of California

Which Whale Moves the Fastest?

There are no Olympics for whales, so no one knows for sure how fast a whale can sprint if it really wants to. Biologists who study whales must estimate their speeds by watching them in the wild.

Fin whales are known for being excellent swimmers. They are sleek and shaped like a torpedo. They have less blubber for their size and more muscle than blue whales. Fin whales are called the "greyhounds of the sea" and are the second largest baleen whale after blue whales. Over short distances, fin whales reach speeds of 20 miles (32 kilometers) per hour.

Sei whales are another fast whale, long and lean like fin whales. Sei whales are known for explosive sprints. By some accounts, sei whales can swim 30 miles (48 kilometers) per hour over short distances, making them faster than dolphins.

Blue whales are also strong swimmers, almost as fast as sei and fin whales.

Fin whales surfacing

57

How Do Scientists Study Whales?

Studying whales is a challenge. They live underwater and are constantly on the move.

All sorts of basic biological information about whales can be difficult to gather. Whales are so huge, it is nearly impossible to weigh them in the wild. Males and females look very similar.

Whales also make noises that people cannot hear. It takes special equipment to listen to whales' calls and songs. Yet another challenge, a blue whale may live 50, 60, or even more than 70 years, which is much longer than the span of a biologist's career.

Despite these obstacles, biologists do study whales. They observe them from boats and also from planes. More recently, scientists have begun tagging whales and using satellites to track their movements. From the satellite data, scientists can see how far a whale swims in a day and how deep it dives. They can also follow its migration routes and its behaviors at night.

Researcher with
humpback whale

Are Baleen Whales in Danger?

Sadly, baleen whales are in danger. Industrial whaling fleets in the 1800's and 1900's slaughtered too many whales. Some species may never recover. Blue, fin, humpback, and right whales are all in danger of becoming extinct.

Through an international pact, most countries, including the United States, no longer hunt whales. A few, such as Norway and Japan, still do.

Whaling, however, is not the only human activity that makes the seas unsafe for whales. Ships and boats sometimes collide with whales. Whales can also become entangled in fishing nets and drown. Other dangers to whales include the overfishing of krill by humans and pollution in ocean waters.

Not all whales are endangered. Some have been able to recover from the era of whaling. The gray whale has been one success story. It was recently removed from the U.S. endangered species list.

Blue whale swimming
with dolphin

Baleen Whale Fun Facts

→ There are fats inside the bones of a baleen whale that help the whale to float.

→ A mother baleen whale has muscles that pump milk into her baby's mouth.

→ Early scientists called baleen whales "mustached whales," because their baleen made the animals look like they had mustaches.

→ Unlike most mammals, whales are hairless. They still, however, get lice. Lice live among the barnacles on a whale's skin or in the folds around the whale's eyes and throat.

→ Whale milk is very fattening. A blue whale calf can gain 9 pounds (4 kilograms) an hour while nursing.

→ Gray whales don't have a fin on their back. Instead, they have ridges on their back that look like giant knuckles.

Glossary

baleen A large, hairy plate that hangs down from a whale's upper jaw and is used to strain out food from water.

baleen whale Type of whale that has plates of baleen in its mouth.

blowhole The opening at the top of a whale's head through which it inhales and exhales air.

blubber The layer of fat that lies under the skin of whales, protecting them from cold.

breach To leap out of the water.

breeding season The time of year during which male and female animals mate.

bubble net A curtain of bubbles that a whale makes to trap prey.

calf A young whale.

copepod Microscopic animal eaten by many whales.

krill Small, shrimplike animal eaten by many whales.

lobtailing When a whale slaps its tail on the surface of the water.

mammal Type of animal in which the female gives birth to live young; a newborn mammal drinks its mother's milk.

migrate To travel from one region to another with a change in the season.

navel The "belly button"—where the umbilical cord was attached.

population A group of animals of the same kind living in the same area.

prey Animals that are hunted and eaten by other animals.

rorquals A family of whales that have long ridges on their throats.

spout The blast of moist air that comes out of a whale's blowhole when it exhales.

toothed whale Type of whale that has teeth.

umbilical cord The tube through which a mammal receives oxygen and nutrients while in its mother's womb.

63

Index

(**Boldface** indicates a photo, map, or illustration.)

baleen, 6, 10, 52, **53**
baleen whales, 6; birth of, 30; colors of, 44; communication by, 38, **39**, 48, 58; endangered, 60; fun facts on, 62; groups of, 32, **33**; gulper, 20; habitats of, 8; identifying, 10; origin of, 34; parts of, 12, **13**; rorqual, 6, 20; senses of, 24; sizes of, 12; skimmer, 20; sleeping by, 42, **43**; speed of, 56; spouting by, 36, **37**; study of, 58, **59**; water sources for, 40
baleen whales, species of: bowhead, 6, 8, 20, 44, **45,** 52; Bryde's, 8; fin, 6, 56, **57**; minke, 6, 16, 20; sei, 6, 20, **31,** 56. *See also* blue whales; gray whales; humpback whales; right whales
barnacles, 44, 52
blowholes, 6, 10, 34
blows. *See* spouts
blubber, 6, 12, 22, 40
blue whales, 6, **7, 35, 41, 61**; body temperature of, 22, **23**; colors of, 44; communication by, 38; dangers to, 26, 60;

eating by, 18, 20, **21**, 28; groups of, 32; habitats of, 8, **9**; nursing by, 28, **29**; relatives and origin of, 34; senses of, 24; size of, 14, **15**; speed of, 56; spouting by, 36, **37**
brain, of whale, 12, 42
breaching, **7**, 38, 50, **51**
bubble nets, 46, **47**

calves: blue-whale, 26, **27, 28, 29**; sei whale, **31**
courtship, 38, 48, **49**

dolphins, 10, **61**

fish, 10, 40, 46

gray whales, 6, 52, 62; colors of, 44; eating by, 20; groups of, 32; hunting of, 60; migration by, 54, **55**; spouting by, 36

humpback whales, 6, **11, 25**, 52; colors of, 44; courtship of, 48, **49**; danger to, 60; eating by, 20, 46, **47**; groups of, 32, **33**; lobtailing by, **39**; sleeping by, **43**; study of, **59**; "wings" of, 50, **51**
hunting. *See* whaling

krill, 18, **19**, 20, **21**, 40, 46

lice, 52, 62
lobtailing, 38, **39**

migration, 8, **9**, 38, 54, 58
milk, whale, 28, 62

navel, of whale, 30

right whales, 6, 20, 32; baleens of, 52, **53**; color of, 44; danger to, 60; pygmy, 6, 16, **17**; spouting by, 36
rorquals, 6, 20

sharks, 10, 26
sleeping, 42, **43**
songs, 48, 58
spouts, 36, **37**

tail movements, 10
teeth, 6, 34

umbilical cord, 30

vocalizations, 38, 58

whales, 6; killer, 26; toothed, 6, 10. *See also* baleen whales
whaling, 26, 60

For more information about Blue Whales and Other Baleen Whales, try these resources:

Whales, by Theresa Greenaway, Raintree Steck-Vaughn, 2001.

Whales, an Eyewitness Book, Dorling Kindersley, 2004.

Big Blue, by Shelly Gill, Charlesbridge Publishing, 2003.

http://www.cetacea.org/
http://seawifs.gsfc.nasa.gov/ocean_planet.html
http://whale.wheelock.edu/Welcome.html

Baleen Whale Classification

Scientists classify animals by placing them into groups. The animal kingdom is a group that contains all the world's animals. Phylum, class, order, and family are smaller groups. Each phylum contains many classes. A class contains orders, an order contains families, and a family contains individual species. Each species also has its own scientific name. (The abbreviation "spp." after a genus name indicates that a group of species from a genus is being discussed.) Here is how the animals in this book fit in to this system.

Animals with backbones and their relatives (Phylum Chordata)

Mammals (Class Mammalia)

Whales (Order Cetacea)

Baleen whales (Suborder Mysticeti)

Bowhead and right whales (Family Balaenidae)
Bowhead whale . . . . *Balaena mysticetus*
Right whales . . . . *Eubalaena* spp.

Gray whale (Family Eschrichtiidae)
Gray whale. . . . . *Eschrichtius robustus*

Pygmy right whale (Family Neobalaenidae)
Pygmy right whale. . . . . *Caperea marginata*

Rorquals (Family Balaenopteridae)
Blue whale . . . . *Balaenoptera musculus*
Fin whale . . . . *Balaenoptera physalus*
Minke whale. . . . . *Balaenoptera acutorostrata*
Sei whale . . . . *Balaenoptera borealis*
Bryde's whale. . . . . *Balaenoptera edeni*
Humpback whale . . . . *Megaptera novaeangliae*

Toothed whales (Suborder Odontoceti)

Dolphins, killer whales, and relatives (Family Delphinidae)

Narwhals and belugas (Family Monodontidae)

Porpoises (Family Phocoenidae)